# ABANDONED
# ALASKA

## COPPER, GOLD, AND RUST

PAUL SCANNELL

AMERICA
THROUGH TIME®
ADDING COLOR TO AMERICAN HISTORY

*For my mum and dad*

America Through Time is an imprint of Fonthill Media LLC
www.through-time.com
office@through-time.com

Published by Arcadia Publishing by arrangement with Fonthill Media LLC
For all general information, please contact Arcadia Publishing:
Telephone: 843-853-2070
Fax: 843-853-0044
E-mail: sales@arcadiapublishing.com
For customer service and orders:
Toll-Free 1-888-313-2665

www.arcadiapublishing.com

First published 2020

ISBN 978-1-63499-217-6

Typeset in Trade Gothic 10pt on 15pt
Printed and bound in England

# CONTENTS

# ABOUT THE AUTHOR

**D**ublin born photographer Paul Scannell is most inspired by misty, moody scenery and derelict sites of industry. An avid lover of rain and never more himself than in brisk icy air, his work increasingly draws him north. In the summer of 2016, he left his life in London to explore Alaska's wilderness, his travels eventually finding him in America's largest national park, the Wrangell St. Elias. He achieved placement on a season-long artist's residency which allowed him to explore a unique landscape rich in untouched human history. His photography has featured extensively in the United Kingdom press and in a number of international art publications. He has exhibited in Dublin and London and after a successful residency in Northwest Iceland, will return to Alaska to further immerse himself in its unique frontier heritage. To see more of his work visit PaulScannellPhotography on Instagram and Wordpress.

Author Portrait

# FOREWORD

Each of us sees something different in a ghost town. All of us see ourselves, though. The first big tourist boom reaching the ghost towns of the American West, in the 1920s, was pushed by a wave of nostalgia for the vanishing frontier—the glories of the expansionist era, the dreams that came true and then died. Later, in the atomic bomb age, tourists saw the end of civilization, or the overreach of capitalism. Historians today see sweeping social and economic forces. Philosophers see the malaise of ruin-obsession. Scavengers see tools to reuse. Environmentalists see hope in the return of nature. Storytellers see ghosts.

In Alaska, the boomers showed up a generation later. The cold dry climate has helped preserve what they left behind. Visitors today see a cautionary political allegory in the ruins. Will the continued reliance on natural resource booms leave Alaska busted flat someday, a ghost state?

Paul Scannell sees heartbreak. He comes to the ghost mining towns of Alaska in a forlorn state of mind, and finds, through his art, a way to express the pain of loss and time's passage. As he explains here, his ache to connect with his own past inspired him to evoke the lost world of the miners. Their tenacity on the cliffs excites him, and yet even these hardy men could not hold on. The immense emptiness of the Wrangell Mountains surrounds these photographs like a summons to eternity. One can almost hear the tread of the miners as they depart—or are those the footsteps of his father?

Yet there is exhilaration in these photos, in the call of summits, in the spirit of his own exploration and discovery. And in the transformative power of an artist's work. Scannell scrambles to find and capture the ideal image, the artifact and the angle, the right moody light, testing himself in collapsing buildings where movement was like fighting his way through a sinking ship, where he was held aloft at times by nothing more than "unwavering faith in century-old, unmaintained joinery."

From the wilderness of Alaska, Scannell has brought back a portrait of a place where despair and hope are cinched tightly together and held fast, like these last buildings cabled to cliffs, poised on the brink of oblivion.

Tom Kizzia

Alaska writer Tom Kizzia is the author of *Pilgrim's Wilderness*, *The Wake of the Unseen Object*, and a forthcoming history of McCarthy and Kennecott during their "lost decades" as ghost towns. He has written for *The New Yorker* magazine, and was a long-time reporter for the *Anchorage Daily News*.

# ACKNOWLEDGMENTS

**WITH SPECIAL THANKS** to Patt Garrett, Neil Darish and my Uncle John. Your support and encouragement guided my journey.

On wild winter nights when a blizzard raged, the bunkhouse shuddered and groaned like a ship weathering heavy seas and the windows rattled at every furious gust.

(Ted Lambert, *The Man Behind the Paintings* (2012), p. 140)

# INTRODUCTION

Alaska's ghost towns are frozen in time, quite literally. Remote and wild, they battle the harshest conditions, hidden under snow for up to nine months a year. Over the first four decades of the twentieth century, Kennecott and McCarthy grew from an endless icy wilderness to the nucleus of the world-famous Kennecott copper industry. At peak production the area was home to around 1,000 people. With the closing of the mine in 1938 and the cessation of rail services, the region became cut-off. The population dwindled and its once-mighty buildings were left to the elements.

Packing up my life in London after the death of my father, I travelled through the United States on a self-guided Greyhound bus tour. Disorientated from grief, I eventually edged my way north to Alaska, drawn by its vastness. It became an instinctual journey driven by kind encounters and a desire to capture the landscape around me. Settling in a tent in the Wrangell St. Elias National Park, I explored distant derelict cabins, precariously perched glacier-side bunkhouses and creepy industrial sites. Each new adventure was undertaken with animated zeal and, all too often, inappropriate hiking apparel.

In hindsight, it is no coincidence that at a time of loss, I was compelled to seek out these broken places. With my own foundations so uncertain, their uneven surfaces afforded me kinship. Their walls gifted me stories of people long-gone. Personal human effects, lying frozen, untouched for a century, connected me to the past in an extraordinarily immersive way. And it was in the past that my mind needed to be.

This book is the culmination of four years of my work, documenting some of America's most prolific frontier history. It is a testament to my love of Alaska and of derelict places and the precious human history they preserve. My research led me, amongst other wonderful books, to the writings of celebrated artist, Ted Lambert. After walking the final 200 miles to McCarthy in 1924, he wrote an inspiring account of his time working in the mines.

Given my fear of heights and general haplessness, my fellow hikers were regularly required to offer considerable levels of encouragement and assistance. I chose them wisely and I'm forever grateful for their help. Thank you to Charlotte, Ben, Jeremy, Mark, Emer, Emma and Dianne for your knowledge and guidance. A special mention must also go to my friends from Wrangell Mountain Air who kindly facilitated my backcountry expeditions. Seeking an airborne exterior shot of the Erie mine, I directed the pilot as we circled the Kennicott Glacier in a 1961 Cessna. I felt like the Irish Indiana Jones. These mountains, glaciers and ghost towns awoke my spirit. With my path so rarely distinct, they paved my journey and lead me to healing. When immersed back in city life, I often daydream of my wild adventures and the joy that I rediscovered. Surrounded by the chaos of urban dwelling, my mind drifts to what remains of Alaska's frozen history—to its mountains of copper, to a century of rust and to rivers of gold.

# 1

# BONANZA

"Is it safe?" I spluttered. The remains of the Bonanza mine sat across a steep scree cliff. I had lugged my camera equipment on a spirited upward hike with the intention of documenting the infamous structure. As though answering my question, the building, with seemingly comic timing, expelled two vast planks from its disheveled innards. Plunging helplessly down the cliff face, they pierced the mountain-top silence with a succession of bellowing thuds. The resulting landslide echoed like an avalanche across the Kennicott Glacier. At that moment, I felt an exterior photograph would suffice.

With the demand for electricity rising stratospherically in the late nineteenth century, copper became a highly sought-after commodity. Fabled mountains of the precious mineral spurred explorative expeditions to Alaska's frozen north. It was on such an adventure that Clarence Warner and Jack Smith discovered Kennecott's "Bonanza" copper deposit in 1900. They had initially mistaken the abundant green surface-malachite for grass horse feed. The mine was developed from 1911 on an east-facing slope of Bonanza Ridge, at an elevation of roughly 6,000 ft. The ever-shifting movements of the adjoining glacier required surface buildings to be cabled to the cliffs for security.

Following three years of gnawing regret, I returned to venture along the scree and challenge myself to brave the interior of the remaining tramway terminal. Entering these buildings involves more than a touch of trepidation and unwavering faith in century-old, unmaintained joinery. They creak with your footsteps and shift with the wind. The sound of water trickles through gaps and crevices, reminding you the shell has been infiltrated and the structure weakened. Although I am cautious, indeed precious by nature, something wild happens to me inside these dilapidated spaces—a sort of daredevil panic to capture and document, even if it means risking life and limb.

The charred remains of a four-story bunkhouse, intentionally set ablaze to reduce liability, lay grotesquely fused with the landscape. I climbed through the rubble with my usual awkward flair, pausing on a raised wooden platform to enjoy rare level ground. Weather-bleached scraps of denim dungarees lay ripped and crumpled in the scorching summer sun. Their rusted buttons spilled dark orange dots throughout the fabric. I clambered onward over mounds of upward facing nails and jagged wood to reach the building that had previously expelled its wooden guts to my terror. Its eastern end jutted over the steeply descending cliff side, supplying a mountain-top vista stretching hundreds of miles.

Stumbling further inward I found thick log floorboards growing spongy and sodden with decades of the freeze-melt cycle. The dank air of a hundred winters hung thick like clay. A large mound of still-frozen snow stubbornly fought the summer temperatures. Hidden from the sun's warmth, it would likely survive until fresh snowfall in late autumn. The central floor space caved toward the middle, the weight of the clunky machinery dragging it to oblivion. Random gaps in the floorboards offered a glimpse of the cliff far below. An open suitcase sat devoid of its contents, as though abandoned mid-packing. At peak production, the mine employed around seventy men. The copper ore was transported from the mine to the terminal building before being loaded and sent for processing, via tram, to the mill in Kennecott. It was laborious, physical work in the most challenging conditions.

With my lenses given a workout, I paused for lunch and sat quietly, imagining the sounds of toil and industry. The amphitheater-like shape of the surrounding cliffs reported the sound of approaching hikers, their observations being transmitted like a radio signal. They playfully discussed the creepiness of the "ghost house" they were approaching. As I covertly listened to their excitement, my eyes settled on a central pillar, eerily adorned with the empty gloves of Bonanza's dead workers. Their ghosts were waiting for them.

Tramway Terminal

Interior Snow Mound

Craggy Mountain Peaks

Tramway Terminal—Front

Bonanza Mine

Tramway Tower

General Electric Crank

View from Tramway Terminal

Ripped Dungarees

Empty Suitcase

Pillar of Gloves

Loading Area

Bunk Room

*Left:* Snowy Locker Room

*Below:* Frozen Rag

Rusted Wheelbarrow

Chugach Mountains

Tramway Terminal—Side view

Tramway Terminal from Above

Gloves—Close up

# 2

# McCARTHY

Corks popped and there were sounds of revelry through the night and into the next day as the town ruffled its hair, stomped its feet, and whooped.

(Lambert, 2012, p63)

"It's the copper in the hills," an impressively bearded local exclaimed. "It attracts all these positive vibes." My Alaskan travels found me residing in a tent on the outskirts of this remote, barely inhabited township. With the cessation of local mining in 1938, McCarthy, once a center of liquor and illicit services, became a relative ghost town. Founded in the early 1900s next to the turntable which orientated copper-laden trains from Kennecott, the town sits below the lofty peaks of Fireweed, Blackburn and Porphyry Mountains.

The burgeoning copper and gold mining industries of the early twentieth century saw an influx of fortune hunters from across the globe. The nearby, conservatively run mining town of Kennecott was alcohol-free, allowing McCarthy to establish itself as a place of booze and bustle for the working men. Fiercely defensive of its freedoms, the town flouted prohibition rules. An early-warning system was devised to announce government officials long in advance of their arrival, giving locals time to safely conceal their moonshine. It was a freewheeling, rough-and-ready den of frontier iniquity.

Miners from the surrounding camps would travel to town for whiskey and women, all too often losing their hard-earned wages to poker. Kate Kennedy, local entrepreneur and madame of McCarthy's whorehouse, supplied a dog-sled taxi service which guaranteed miners an evening of debauchery and passage back in time for shift. Those too drunk for the return journey could sleep it off in the town's jail, lest they freeze in the snow.

With the Kennecott mine's closing, the town's population reduced in an instant. The ensuing stoppage of rail services left those that remained stranded, and the town unreachable. Empty buildings were left to the brutal winters and pilfered mercilessly as they decayed. A fire in the 1940s caused widespread destruction, further reducing the population to less than fifty hardy souls. By the 1970s, fewer than ten people remained.

As the weather drifted to autumn, my tent blew away in a violent gale, luckily without me inside it. I had also melted my hiking boots in a misguided attempt at drying them on a barrel stove. I sought refuge in a creaky guest room on the upper floor of the old hardware store. Built in 1911, it lay abandoned from the early 1940s, eventually undergoing stabilization in 1976. It is currently home to the Wrangell Mountains Centre, an outward looking non-profit organization. Its dusty rooms and corridors are like a time machine. Every morning I would peer through my bedroom window to the remains of the Golden Hotel. Once a vibrant watering hole, part of its original bar was removed, weakening the structure irreparably. The building sat empty for decades, tilting ever-more acutely, until finally collapsing in the winter of 2016 from the weight of snow. With it went another chapter of the town's history.

Against the harshest of conditions, the passing of time and remoteness of the landscape, McCarthy survives and prospers. Steering clear of "Disneyfication," its authenticity avoids the dreaded vintage caricature that befalls many historical places. The town's past and present are intrinsically fused and dependent on one another. Newer structures sit seamlessly next to their older ramshackle counterparts. Bed frames, wagon wheels, tin cans and rusted trucks are mindfully refashioned and reused. My melted hiking boots have proudly joined the town's hodgepodge of recycled flowerpots, most recently hosting Grandma Patt's lovely yellow marigolds. This is a town kept alive by its welcoming of wanderers, its generosity of spirit, its sharing of stories and its libertarian soul.

The Old Hardware Store

The Road to Kennecott

Smashed-Up Truck

Peeling Paint

McCarthy Cabin

*Above:* The Old Golden

*Right:* "Patience"

Kate Kennedy's Cabin

The Old Golden and Loy Green's Cabin

McCarthy Aurora

# 3

# JUMBO

Located in 1900, the Jumbo orebody was the second to be developed on Bonanza Ridge. As with the earlier Bonanza site, the larger mine buildings were set on rollers and anchored to the cliffs for security. My first hike to the area brought me up a steep mountain trail, passing wooden tram towers, still supporting vast steel cables after a century of unmaintained exposure. The immediate approach to the site was awash with evidence of its past human inhabitants.

Tin cans, broken glass bottles, cooking utensils and dismembered spades lay strewn. Thick stubborn mounds of snow buried much of the site. Placing your full weight on these patches could mean sinking onto nails or sharp metal. An area on the upper rim hosted kindly placed artifacts. A lady's leather boot, lightbulbs, lumps of malachite and unidentifiable clothing all lay fused with rubble and ice, like an open-air museum piece. The collection sat under a sign politely urging those inclined toward pilfering to reconsider.

With the tramway completed by 1915, the site comprised four bunkhouses, a blacksmith shop, transformer house and various storage sheds. The recreational hall had a card room and gym and even hosted movies twice a week. Its only remaining bunkhouse, once four stories, has partially collapsed, leaving the upper floors tilting perilously. Fumbling up the steep inward climb, I found bunkrooms on either side, each hosting metal bed frames, warped from the structural collapse. Sodden fluff leaked from century-old mattresses like soggy entrails. The sharply increasing angle of my climb disorientated my internal spirit level. Pulling myself upward with the edge of each door frame, I felt as though I was fighting my way through a sinking ship. In hindsight, these chaotic surfaces resonated perfectly with me. Their dangerous uncertainty made unexpected sense.

Pausing for photographs, I stopped at each doorway, angling my neck left and right to find balance. The manically misshapen window frames left me unsure of how to position my camera. It was like a creepy carnival funhouse. I fought my way to the light at the far end of the hall and stood atop the mangled shambles of weather-beaten wood. Rust spilling from each snow-covered mound was reflected in the craggy orange-tinged cliffs above. There, I could appreciate the indelible power time and weather hold over these fragile places. The eighty winters since desertion have created a hybrid space—half from nature, half from man and they are each in constant conflict. It is Alaska's intention to reclaim its territory. It appears Alaska will win the battle.

Collapsed Bunkhouse

Rust-Stained Fabric

Bed Through a Window Frame

Lady's Boot

Sardine Can

Bunkhouse—Side View

Workshop and Misty Mountain

Bunkhouse Window Frame

Bunk Interior

Ceiling Beams on a Mattress

Rusty Tin Can

Detached Side Wall

Bunkhouse Roof

Metal and Stone

Twin Bunk Room

Ice and Rust

Single Glove

Man's Leather Shoe

Creepy Carnival Funhouse

Jumbo Bunkhouse

End of the Tramway

Collapsed Ceiling Beams

Tram Tower

Lightbulb Moment

Tram Tower with Cables

# 4

# KENNECOTT

Kennecott was the "end of the line" for the famous Copper River Northwestern Railway, an unrivalled feat of engineering that took 6,000 men nearly five years to complete. Blasting almost 200 miles through mountains and glaciers, it enabled the region's copper industry to flourish. It was the operational heart of the Jumbo, Erie, Bonanza, Glacier and Motherlode copper mines. A clerical misspelling led to two variants developing in tandem. "Kennecott" relates to the town and mine while "Kennicott" refers to the river and glacier. The twentieth century saw the area evolve from wilderness to bustling industrial center to ghost town. Over recent decades the town and its surroundings have become a tourist attraction for those willing to brave the bumpy sixty-mile journey along the infamous McCarthy Road.

Originally overlooked by the towering Kennicott Glacier, the site peers west toward Donoho Peak, over a vast expanse of glacial moraine. Its upward-sprawling mill building spans fourteen stories and its hospital boasted Alaska's first x-ray machine. Global copper prices plummeted in 1937, leading to the mill's closure the following year. The last train left on November 11, 1938, taking with it the lion's share of the remaining workers. The town's population, listed as 494 in the 1920 census, by 1940 had fallen to just five. Current stabilization efforts aim not to sanitize the site, rather to prevent further deterioration, allowing future generations to immerse themselves in an authentic historical mining district. Kennecott was designated a National Historic Landmark in 1986.

Hitching a ride from nearby McCarthy on the back of a motorcycle, I first visited the town close to dusk. The sun's disappearing glow set the surrounding snowy peaks on fire. The remains of the hospital and east bunkhouse are both considered past saving. Water from National Creek gushes past their protuberant ground floors. I set my tripod on a raised spot above both buildings and watched the sun sink. Its shadows danced over the glacial moraine, changing the hue from burnt orange to crimson. If I let it, maybe the end of the line could bring me somewhere new.

East Annex

Top of Kennecott Mill Building

Kennecott Powerhouse

View Over Glacial Moraine

Mill Building Exterior

Locker room—West Bunkhouse

*Left:* Upper Corridor—West Bunkhouse

*Below:* Bunkroom with Glacial View—West Bunkhouse

Kennecott Leaching Plant

Sunset over the Root Glacier

# 5

# ERIE

I first saw the remains of the Erie Mine in the summer of 2016. Descending over the Root Glacier in a two-seater Cessna, I caught a glimpse of the partially collapsed structure, perched on a cliff edge 1,200 ft. above the glacier. Completed in 1924, the building, aptly known as the "Eagle's nest," was left to the elements with the closing of the Kennecott copper mine. Local folklore says the working men were given just days to vacate their homes. Warned of an imminent final outward train, they gathered what they could, leaving posters hanging on walls, plates on tables and linen on beds.

The miners had been transported to and from the site by tram, a metal bucket suspended on cables which could be winched over great heights and distances. With the mechanism long dismantled, the only way to this mountain-top Marie Celeste was on foot, climbing above the barracks and scaling down Bonanza's steep north-westerly face. Afraid of heights and often excessively vocal, I tackled the terrifying ascent with the kind encouragement of two locals. Braving a final razor-thin ledge, I fell to the ground with grateful profanity. I had passed the test and now the reward.

The building's front aspect is breathtaking. Donohoe Peak lies opposite, its ancient limestone slabs slicing diagonally downward to the icy waves of the Kennecott Glacier. We entered the building to the rear to find a mess-hall, mostly intact. Part of the ceiling lay buckled downward, spewing an upper corridor to the ground floor. The rear wall caved inward, being nudged ever closer to infinity by the mountain behind. A bunk room on my left rewarded me with a dual aspect glacier-scape. Its empty bunkbeds peered outward through glassless windows. A brisk, icy wind circulated the smell of musty wood. Blood-like rust spilled from the grubby wooden wall slats.

Beyond the mess-hall lay a dark pantry, its shelves empty except for a dusty rag, left part-suspended. The kitchen's roof had also buckled downward, rendering the room impenetrable. Food is life and both were gone. A further social space beyond hosted a chaotic array of broken chairs and barrel heaters. In the decades proceeding abandonment, local residents often travelled to Kennecott's mines for furniture and utensils—dubbing their loot "kenni-crap." Rumor has it that Erie's pool table, having become home to a family of mountain goats, was taken from this room and slid down the mountain.

During the brutal winter of 1927, Ted Lambert wrote of starting the year "painting frost patterns inside the windowpanes." His descriptions of working in the mine tell of a bleak place made bearable by the comradery of his fellow workers. Simply put, "you worked like a horse, ate like a pig, and slept like a bear." These walls saw brawls and banter over many long winters. This room was a place of sanctuary and conversation where backgrounds blurred and brotherly bonds were built. Half-burnt candles that once cast the shadows of their midnight card games sat permanently extinguished, their wicks damp and charred.

Moving to an upper floor, I tread the stairs carefully, allowing rain drops to guide me from the wettest boards. Human effects lay scattered on the landing. A moldy blanket that once soothed aching shivers lay partially fused to the rotting floor. A flopped rubber boot echoed century-old footsteps, ready for battle and weary from work. I paused at the frame of each consecutive door and imagined faces peering to a whitewash wilderness. In the corner of a rear-facing bunk room we found the tiniest scrap of a poster clinging defiantly to the wall. The eyes of an unidentifiable 1930s starlet peered downward, her gaze forever frozen, her oglers long-gone.

The far side of the corridor offered two more doorways to front facing rooms. Both spaces were missing their ceiling and front wall, like a giant doll's house. Beds that hosted homesick dreams lay strewn with debris and open to the elements. I was, perhaps, not on the top or the edge of the world, but somewhere close to both. With dusk approaching, we retraced our trusted steps and returned to McCarthy to tell of our findings. When I hear the Erie bunkhouse has finally succumbed, I will feel yet more proud to have walked its creepy corridors. Metal rusts, wood rots and people die, but it's in these darkest corners I was finding the most connection, and rarely so more than in this "Eagles Nest."

Erie Bunkhouse

Mess Hall with Collapsed Upper Floor

Erie Bunkhouse and Donoho

Erie Bunkhouse Fly-By

Bedframe

Heating Valve

Randrops on Metal

Social Room

Social Room—Rear View

Glacierscape

Candles, Chair and Barrel Stove

Lightbulb and Jam Jar

Rusty Bedframe

Bunkroom—Long View

Single Bunkroom

Rubber Boot

Rusty Bunks

Plimsoll

Room with a View

Poster Girl

Erie Mine Adit

Above the Eagle's Nest

Storage Shed and Glacier

Erie Bunkhouse—Aerial Shot

# 6

# BREMNER

The abandoned Bremner gold mining district is as far-flung as to appear remote to McCarthy, itself a tiny speck in Alaska's 20,000-square-mile Wrangell St. Elias National Park. Nestled in the Chugach Mountain range, the site's inaccessibility ensures a near pristine example of pre-WWII mining history. Aside from a lengthy and dangerous hike through dense brush, the only way to visit the site is by air. As the bush plane retreats, becoming a dot against the landscape, you can't help but feel abandoned. With us we had bug dope, pepper aerosol to deter bear attacks and special food storage canisters with opening mechanisms too complicated for large mammals—including myself.

The buildings of the Yellowband Camp are a mix of log-built "balloon frame" and corrugated sheet metal. The operation went into production in 1935 and comprised a bunkhouse, storage shed, garage, assay shed and hydroelectric plant. In 1942, gold was declared a non-essential mineral leading to a stoppage of mining for the rest of the war. Production levels failed to recover, leaving the site mostly untouched.

Whilst there you're alone, except for the bears, eagles, marmots and an odd species of ground squirrel, whose aggressive friendliness can be alarming at times. They're eating Bremner's abandoned buildings one plank at a time, scurrying under the floorboards as you find the courage to walk further into the shadows. The sudden noise of their brazen scuttling startled more than one long exposure.

Pulling the thick pin from each makeshift clasp, I dragged heavy log doors to reveal irresistible rags and riches. Spades, screws and all manner of discarded tools lay mostly where they were left. A 1920s Ford Model-A truck peeked out from the darkness of the garage. Many of its 68,000 miles were spent ferrying ore from the nearby Sheriff Mine to the Lucky Girl Mill. Jagged rust holes in the walls of the adjoining workshop let morning sunlight slice sharply inward, illuminating more trinkets from the gloom. Impressive cobwebs danced in the breeze of the gaps.

To witness light still travelling around these sad interiors was somehow reassuring.

My childhood family Sundays were spent trudging through fields to the sound of raindrops tapping on my hood. With my father leading the convoy, we'd hike Dublin's mountains, forests, parks and piers. Those precious formative moments, albeit mostly spent complaining of sore legs and hunger, had unknowingly taught us an enduring appreciation of nature. It was perhaps his greatest gift to us.

Exploring Bremner's surrounding peaks, I hiked upward alongside the hydroelectric pipes and sat by a barely-standing penstock. Allowing my thoughts to slow to the pace of the landscape, I watched clouds glide over a wide valley floor filled with flowers, birch scrub and alpine meadows. I had never been so removed from the world, yet so connected to it. I thought of those distant childhood Sundays. The past and its people were everywhere. In Bremner, the present didn't need to exist at all.

Garage Workshop

Workshop Interior

Ford Model A

Storage Shed

Workshop Shelf

Ground Squirrel

Oil-Burning Lantern

Bunkhouse and Storage Shed

Rusted Hinge

Horse Shoe

Hydroelectric Powerhouse Interior

Nuts

Ford Model A—Interior

Hydroelectric Generator

Hydroelectric Gauge

Lumberjack Shirt

Hills Bros Coffee Can

Freight Wagon

Wooden Penstock Tower

Rusty Nails in Wood

Bremner Hydroelectric Powerhouse

# 7

# CHITITU

"Enjoy the rust porn," our pilot shouted from the Cessna, as it trundled back up May Creek's grass airstrip. We were four miles from Chititu, an abandoned gold mining camp and the subject of much whiskey-fueled folklore. "There's something up there," warned my drinking companion. These bar-side tales of haunted noises had inspired me to investigate. With twenty-four hours to navigate the hike and return for our scheduled pick-up, we trudged from the airstrip, deeper into bear country.

Chititu, originally settled in 1902 as part of Alaska's gold rush, sits at the confluence of Rex and Chititu Creeks. At its peak, it was home to around fifty miners, and comprised several log-built offices and bunkhouses, a cookhouse, bathhouse and a maintenance shop. With the closing of the Copper River and Northwestern Railway, large scale mining ceased. Its remoteness has ensured relative safety from greedy artifact hunters. Winding from riverside to dense canopy, the trail offered glimpses of its mining past. Mounds of rubble, tailings-piles and rock-dumps peppered the landscape.

The old Nizina post office, decommissioned in 1926, sits in the woods above the trail, silently observing the few that pass. Its facade is a shambolic mound of twisted wood and broken glass. Only the rear room remains intact. Furious scratch marks from a curious grizzly bear crown the door frame; its repeated unsuccessful attempts to gain access ominously recorded in the wood. Inside we found a century of human habitation merged curiously. Moth-eaten blankets hung next to mildewed sleeping bags. A book of psalms lay open, "I surrender all." I pictured the room's last occupant, kneeling by his makeshift pew in isolated contemplation, with autumn's first snowflakes falling.

Reaching Chititu, we radiated out in opposite directions, combing the waist-height foliage, like ants looking for food. It was like a terrestrial *Titanic* debris field. Leather horse straps snaked through desiccated leaves toward a shabby wooden doghouse, half-submerged in grass. Our investigations became less skittish with every discovery. The warped door of the cookhouse leaned awkwardly inward, like a host too drunk to greet his guests. Inside, a gaping hole above the kitchen left the range, table and sink open to the weather's turn. The bathhouse spoke of warmth and welcome weekly washes. Wooden beams supporting the workshop's vast metal roof creaked and bent like dusty old bones. A hole had rusted through the metal, mercifully allowing meltwater to relieve the weight each spring.

We prepared our camp, ate food and swigged liquor. As I drifted to slumber, the sound of the creek morphed into distant banter, barely audible cheer, even music. It might be easy to dismiss it as a drunken dream, but I'm not going to. Before setting out to meet our plane, I revisited the site. At the top of a steep incline a large log cabin sat perched, its door ominously ajar. A century of grime on the windowpanes fed the internal murkiness. Drawn inward, I found all four corners cloaked in thick ancient shadows.

Socks hung over the barrel stove, left drying eternally. Every surface spoke of people and their absence. Avoiding the animal scat, I drifted further into the darkness, settling on a ripped mattress. Outside the grubby window, raindrops furiously tapped rusted tin drums with a discordant unity. I closed my eyes and breathed deeply the sweet, pungent smell rising from the straw floor. I had sought out these empty shacks, compelled by their treasures, but it wasn't the remnants of strangers I had been hoping to find. The simplicity of that moment will never leave me.

These forgotten places gave me solace in the dark and a destination when I was lost. I picture their partial structures leaning against vicious winds—as defiantly as my most cherished memories fight the passing of time. It was in their silent shells I could connect with the nature of an impossible loss. None of it was intentional nor my journey planned, but the best things rarely are. With my internal compass pointed north, I found my way to the eagle's nest. Perhaps that bearded McCarthy local was right—maybe there was something magic in the hills; something mysterious and kind. The photos I captured remind me still that light, however faint, finds its way to even the darkest places. And having been to the end of the line, that simple lesson remains every bit as precious as copper, gold or those wild peaks, lost in blizzards and frozen under endless Alaskan ice.

Wrangell Mountain Air Drop-off

A-Frame Log Cabin

Misty Morning Creek View

Grizzly Bear Scratch Marks

Nizina Post Office—Side View

Nizina Post Office—Interior

I Surrender All

Mossy Ceiling Hole

Cooking Pan with Wood Bark

Nizina Post Office—Front View

*Above:* Sunlight on Cracked Windowpane

*Left:* Nizina Post Office—Table Top

Tin Can

Doghouse

Nuts and Bolts

Pantry

Kitchen Counter

Moldy Mattress

*Above:* Rusting Pipe

*Left:* Storage Shed

Cabin in the Woods

California Tomatoes

Rainy Oil Drums

Kitchen Range

*Above:* Bathhouse Exterior

*Right:* Bathhouse Interior

Log Cabin

Rainy Morning Return

*Right:* Socks over Barrell Stove

*Below:* Ripped Straw Mattress

# BIBLIOGRAPHY

Bleakley, G., *In the Shadow of Kennecott: The Forgotten Mining Camps of the Wrangell Mountain Region*

Douglass, W., *A History of the Kennecott Mines, Kennecott Alaska,* (Seattle, Washington, 1964)

Brooks, A., and Others, *Mineral Resources of Alaska, Report on Progress of Investigations,* (Washington Printing Office, Washington, 1921)

Fensterman, G., *Hiking Alaska, Wrangell-St. Elias National Park and Reserve,* (Morris Book Publishing, LLC, USA, 2008)

Lambert, T., edited by Freedman, L., *The Man Behind the Paintings,* (University of Alaska Press, Fairbanks, 2012)

Olsen, S., and Shaine, B. *Community & Copper in a Wild Land,* (The Wrangells Mountain Centre, Alaska, 2005)

White, P., *Cultural Landscape Report: Bremner Historic District,* (The National Park Service, Alaska, 2000)